I Want to Be a Veterinarian!

How to Become [illegible] ds

Natalie Kelli

Table of Contents

Introduction

Have you ever dreamed of working with amazing animals every day? Do you love learning about different creatures and how to keep them healthy and happy? Then you may be perfect for an exciting career as a veterinarian!

Veterinarians are real-life animal superheroes. They use their knowledge of science and medicine to help pets, livestock, and even wild animals. From caring for a kitten with a cold to assisting in a complicated surgery on a sick horse, no two days are ever the same for these animal doctors.

In this book, you'll discover everything you need to know about the world of veterinary medicine and what it takes to pursue this paw-some profession. Get ready to explore:

- The different types of veterinary careers, from working with cute household pets to majestic exotic animals
- The important skills and character traits that make a great veterinarian
- What education and training path you'll need to follow to become an animal doctor
- A behind-the-scenes look at a typical day in the life of several different vets

- Insider tips and advice from real veterinarians on how to achieve your dreams
- Fun facts about the amazing animals that vets get to work with and help every day
- And much more!

So, if you have a passion for animals, science, and helping others, this book is for you! Join us on an exciting journey to learn how you can one day put on that veterinarian's white coat and make a difference in the lives of animals and the people who love them. Let's get started!

Chapter 1

Veterinarian Education Requirements and Career Information

Veterinarians are those people who treat the animals called vet doctors or veterinarians. They need a certain amount of formal education. Veterinarians study in their degree programs related to animals and know the job duties, responsibilities, and licensing requirements to find out if this is the right career for you.

Key points are helpful for a veterinarian.

Some people and parents have always told you that they think you will make a great veterinarian. You think that others assume that this is the right path and that it is based solely on your love and interest in animals.

You are right to think that many take many other specialties to build their career in veterinary medicine. Most essential skills are not developed until you visit a vet school, but some other important features draw you to a career in animal science.

To become a vet specialist, you need to know a lot about education, job duties, salary, and what the future holds for you.

There are a lot of animals in the universe but you will have to choose those which you like more e.g dogs, cats, horses, and a lot more.

Although many people love animals, people love them as much as you love them. Animal care has always made you interested in becoming an animal. Regardless of the passion, your initial interest can be a rewarding career. A veterinarian is responsible for provoking the urge to work with animals.

Veterinarians work with animals and solve problems without being able to talk to them. But being a veterinarian is more than just playing with your favorite pet and doing routine checkups. You may need some business skills or work to improve the relationship. Some things that current practitioners think everyone should know before taking veterinary medicine.

Career path for Veterinary Doctor/ Veterinarian

To become a veterinarian, a student must plan his or her career from the 12th standard. To do this, a student must have a strong background in subjects that include chemistry, biology, and physics. Admission to Veterinary College / Institute is based on the marks obtained in the entrance examination conducted by the concerned authority.

Essential Information

Veterinarians specialize in veterinary medicine, surgery, and treatment. Veterinary program graduates can care for small animals (pets) such as dogs and cats, or specialize in large animals such as horses, cattle, and buffaloes. Because of the increase in the pet industry, the opportunities are expected to grow faster than average in the coming years.

Education Requirements

Vet doctors are required to complete a four-year or five-year degree in the "Doctor of Veterinary Medicine" (DVM) program along with the undergraduate school. It is necessary that these professionals also need to be licensed before practicing in the profession.

Students who wish to enroll in the veterinary program, receive a bachelor's degree in a general science-related field such as biology, science, molecular biology, chemistry, animals, science, and Biochemistry.

However, some students may have difficulty enrolling in veterinary programs without a degree. Students who have not completed undergraduate school typically need to complete at least 45-90 semester credit hours.

Note:

Most universities and colleges have different eligibility criteria for admission to undergraduate programs. While some classes require at least 50%, some universities and colleges require at least 60%. Some colleges/universities also check the age before getting admission.

A bachelor's degree in veterinary sciences can usually be completed in four years. Studies commonly include both theory and lab education. Courses that taught students for veterinary school tend to include:

- Microbiology
- Animal management
- Anatomy and physiology
- Animal nutrition
- Equine care
- Pathology

DVM programs take four to five years to complete an education career. DVM degree is a semester-wise study, not annually.
Students complete two semesters each year. The first segment typically consists of theory sections while the last two years focus on more clinical practices.

Coursework typically includes:

- Animal behavior

- Veterinary pharmacology
- Animal nutrition
- Clinical pathology
- Large and small animal medicine
- Diagnostic imaging
- Anesthesia and surgery principles
- Theriogenology

In clinical practices, students complete rotations and gain maximum knowledge in the clinic. They have to complete rotations in various veterinary specialties, such as domestic animals, dentistry, cardiology, oncology, or equine care. Students learn many skills essential to veterinary medicine, such as how to treat wounds, prescribe medication, perform surgery, and set fractures.

Career Information

Veterinarians try to improve and cure the health of household pets. They also check animals in laboratories, on farms, and in zoos. They have great expertise in treating and diagnosing dysfunctions and diseases in such animals, which may include using preventative measures, surgery, and the use of the latest technology. A good veterinarian spends a great deal of time interacting with pet owners, offering advice on feeding, grooming, and breeding.

While veterinarians are well known for pet care, some work in a private clinic, some know food-animal practices, and provide care for livestock animals like sheep, goats, cattle, buffalo, and pigs. Some vets have a lot of research to prevent humans from contracting the diseases that are carried by animals. Veterinarian duties include using diagnostic tests and lab equipment, setting broken bones, euthanizing chronically ill animals, and birthing animals.

Licensing Information

After earning a DVM degree, aspiring veterinarians now must become licensed, and can do a job anywhere. All states in the USA require veterinarians to pass the North American Veterinary Licensing Exam (NAVLE). Tests consist of a 360-question that lasts 7.5 hours and assesses candidates' knowledge of veterinary sciences and animal species. Some states also have additional procedures, such as passing veterinary law and clinical skills exams.

Salary Information

According to the U.S. Bureau of Labor Statistics (BLS), veterinarians earned a median annual wage of $95,460 in May 2019. The upper 10% earned $160,780 or more than it per year, while the lowest 10% earned $58,080 or less.

Jacksonville Florida was the second-highest-paying city with a reported mean salary of $188,880. Demand for veterinarians is expected to increase by 18% in the future between 2016 and 2026.

Chapter 2

I Wish I Knew Before I Became a Veterinarian

A veterinarian takes almost as much time as becoming a human doctor

You typically do four years of undergraduate and have to complete the prerequisites and required tests to enter into a veterinary college, which is another four years of school. If you decide you want to specialize in the veterinary sciences, you do an internship a residency, or an internship. But even if you ever only plan for a year and three more years of residency after graduation.

As a general practitioner, you do not need to practice on domestic pets, your training encircles all areas of veterinary medicine. So you go to small animals, like dogs and cats, to exotic animals like birds and reptiles, to farm animals, like sheep, cows, and goats. And there are rotations where you're on-call at midnight, where you work on weekends and holidays.

Many people have the impression that you play with dogs and kittens all day and that this is inferior to human medicine. As a veterinarian, I need to know how to specialize in dentistry, surgery, internal medicine, X-rays, and human medicine.

Working with people working with animals is as much a part of this

It depends on owners who need to decide what treatment they want to do or what their budget is, which limits what you can do. And then you have other staff, such as receptionists and technicians, and sometimes you have an outside specialist or veterinarian with whom you have to collaborate. It's surprising how much training you have received with the animals in veterinary school and how much training you get along with people. This is a great learning curve for owners, you, and the pet to evaluate how to communicate effectively.

The most difficult part is to keep pets

It's a really difficult time for the owners to handle this situation. I am trying to present them with every option possible, whether that's additional diagnostics and treatments or hospital care, and try to help them make the best decision for themselves and the pet. If they do decide on euthanasia, I do everything in my hand to make sure it's as dignified as possible.

Most of the time, the owners are right there with the whole procedure. I would tell them exactly what to expect and what is near to happen. And of course, at that time I will cry right along with the owners. I think that most of my grief comes from the loss the owner is facing because I wouldn't perform euthanasia unless I truly believed it was in the best for the pet.

I think I've improved at handling it over the years. I don't think you ever become faint to it, but I also think you become a little more realistic. If we have a cat that is alive until the age of 18, you will appreciate that this cat has lived a wonderful life for 18 years and with a family that loves them.

Some animals will be difficult to handle

I encounter cats every day, and sometimes dogs, which are aggressive and difficult to handle. I'm not more afraid of small dogs or cats because when they try to bite me, it's very easy to control, stop, or use them if necessary. But there are times when I am testing a 100-pound dog that I don't know very well and need a lot of care. To test a dog, you have to be fine with his face, so you have to trust the person who is holding the animal for you.

I realize that maybe 95% of the time when those animals are acting aggressively, it's all based on fear rather than behavioral issues. Pets are nervous because they are in a new environment with new people, and working with them that they do not understand. Because we understand this perspective, we do everything we can to alleviate their fears, take care of them, and make them feel comfortable, and I think that helps a lot.

Pet owners might get offended

Obesity is the biggest health problem in pets and I deal with this kind of thing every day. If the pet is just a little overweight, I try to approach it with a sense of humor and tell them that their pet is a bit of a part. The owner will usually laugh and we will come up with a game plan to fix it. I try to explain to them why being overweight is a concern.

This is not a cosmetic concern. That is, their pets have an increased risk of diabetes and arthritis. Usually, the owners understand when you visit these things, but there are situations where we say the same thing on every visit and the pet is the same. It's very frustrating because I know they are trying their best, and I know that they do not deliberately harm your pet, they love many people. Even when you don't work late, you'll be exhausted.

Time management

I am very lucky to get a job where I can go at 5:30 and get a weekend off. But there are days when it is a very emotional task. You watch meetings from 7:30 a.m. to 5 p.m., and if you're not in a meeting, you're making a phone call. And each of these owners has a different concern and a different priority and you have to be fully engaged for all of them. When I get home, I often get frustrated and have to go as a mother and wife.

You will not always work with kittens and dogs

Common, but we see some guinea pigs, ferrets, hamsters, rabbits, and occasionally birds and lizards for annual examinations. I will do my best even if I am not so familiar with this species. I have all my class notes scanned on my iPad so I can reference them a lot, and I can call the specialist at the nearest foreign animal hospital and ask for their opinion.

If someone is wrong and I think it's out of my comfort zone, I tell them it would be in their best interest to see a specialist, but if they don't want to or can't go, I can help. I will do my best.

Owning a pet will make you a better veterinarian

Our patients can't tell us what's wrong, so I think living with animals in my personal life helps me learn a little more from them. And it helps me understand my client's point of view because I have a lot of pets.

It will be difficult to separate your professional life from your personal life

When we are out in a social environment, I often do not honestly mention that I am a veterinarian because it becomes the focus of the conversation. Even with friends and family, if it's a very engaging conversation, I give them my card and ask to meet them. There must be limits to this so you can still live a private life because animals are made a subject in which most people feel very emotional, especially about their animals.

Preventative medicine is just as important for your pet as it is for you

It is very easy to vaccinate pets every year and send them on their way unless they are due for their next vaccine or a crisis. But if you take the time to ask these additional questions, dig deeper into their medical history, or inform the employer about proper nutrition or lifestyle, it can have such an effect. If you can make rapid changes to your diet, you can improve your pet's and its owner's quality of life.

You will be the pet from beginning to end, and you will be the owner beyond that

As a general practitioner, I like this. One of the reasons is that you can meet people when they come with their new dog on the first day. You are part of that excitement, you are part of teaching them how to take the best care of this dog, you are watching them for a while every month, and then every year. And then it gets to the point where the animal starts to age and you help them take better care of your pet.

And then finally, you will help them live a very peaceful, dignified life, whether it means happiness or something else. I am incredibly committed not only to our patients but also to our employers. You will get to know him and his family and what is happening in their lives.

The most rewarding part of a job is that you make bonds because you see them over and over again. It's not like they pop up once and you never see them again. The majority of our patients return with their next pet two months later, even after losing it.

Chapter 3
Types of Job Roles Veterinary Doctor/ Veterinarian

About Veterinary Doctor/ Veterinarian

A veterinarian is a medical professional who provides treatment to all kinds of animals. Veterinarians fulfill the healthcare requirements of pets, zoos, livestock, wildlife, and laboratory animals. There are various types of vets such as those who work with small animals like cats and dogs pet lovers, those who work with large farm animals such as horses, cows, and goats, and those who work with wild animals such as wolves, lions, giraffes, etc.

Veterinary doctors study to treat all kinds of animals, some choose to take up the treatment of small animals (pet specialists) while some become experts in looking after animals on farms and forests. Most of the veterinary practitioners work in private hospitals and clinics, laboratories, or classrooms. But many have to travel to farms and forests for the welfare of animals.

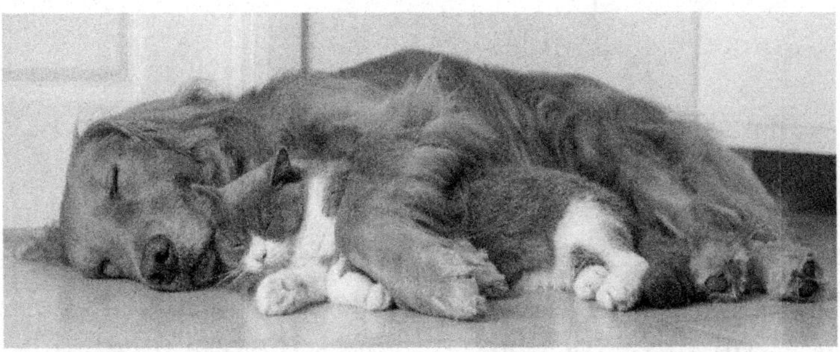

After completing the qualifications, skills, and training, there are a lot of job profiles in this field that you can target based on your interest. Following are some of the popular jobs for Veterinarians:

Companion Animal Veterinarians: Companion animal veterinarians are those who work in private hospitals or clinics and provide their services to pets such as dogs, cats, birds, etc.

Research Veterinarians: Research veterinarians usually work in laboratories and are always involved in research to find new treatments for diseases and surgical techniques.

Equine Veterinarian:

Equine veterinarians are those who provide medical treatment to horses, donkeys, and mules.

Food Safety and Inspection Veterinarians:

They provide inspections for major animal diseases and vaccines for the treatment of animals. They also provide a lot of tests on a livestock farm to check the quality of milk.

They work for animal welfare, do research to improve animal health, and provide government food safety rules. The main purpose of an inspection is to maintain the quality of livestock products and avoid the use of contaminated meat with chronic diseases.

Food Animal Veterinarians

Those veterinarians who treat diseases and injuries of farm animals such as cattle, pigs, ships, and livestock, and educate people about food and other health practices.

Veterinary Dermatologists These types of veterinarians are involved in diagnosing any skin disease that an animal may have and performing biopsies, cultures, and skin scrapings.

Veterinary Pharmacologist

The veterinary pharmacologist deals with the medicine and monitors an animal's progress in veterinary hospitals kept under care.

Public Health (known as Epidemiologists)

These vets work for public health issues, within cities, countries, states, and federal agencies. They help in controlling and preventing animal and human diseases, as well as investigating animal and human disease outbreaks. The U.S. Food and Drug Administration (FDA) employs these veterinarians to find the safety and efficacy of medicines and food additives.

ANESTHESIA AND ANALGESIA

Every licensed veterinarian can administer anesthesia. Veterinary anesthesiologists highly specialize in treating pain and reducing the risk of complications. They make specific plans for each animal, diagnose and deal with problems during surgery, and carefully monitor patients after the procedure.

DENTISTRY

Animals may not care if they have aesthetically pleasing teeth, but healthy choppers are essential for a sustainable life. Dental problems can lead to malnutrition and general anxiety. A veterinary dentist can perform any necessary oral surgery.

EMERGENCY AND CRITICAL CARE

When animals become injured or suddenly develop a serious health problem, they need prompt medical attention. Vet specialists in emergency and critical care are trained for these types of high-pressure situations. In an emergency, vets are equipped with immediate action and make sure the animal gets the attention it needs.

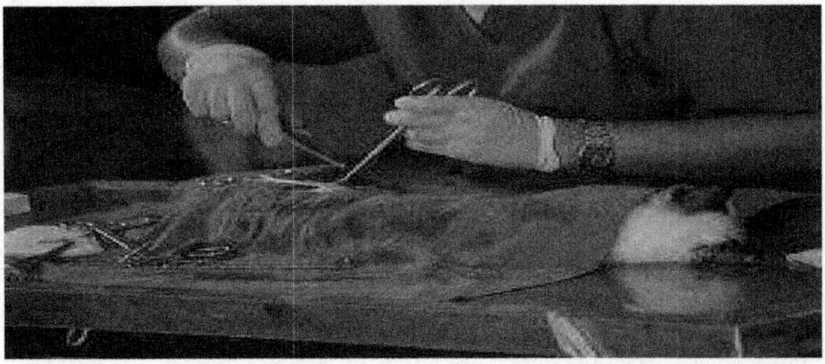

INTERNAL MEDICINE

Highly trained veterinarians treat uncommon or complicated diseases. Pet owners are often referred to these specialists by their regular vet doctors when the case is complicated or when the animal requires a highly technical procedure.

Veterinarians can further specialize in the following:

- Cardiology
- Large animal internal medicine
- Neurology
- Oncology
- Small animal internal medicine

MICROBIOLOGY

Veterinary microbiologists are often the driving force behind preparations for the treatment of infectious animal diseases. They typically work in a lab and try to find the cause of the disease. Microbiologists do their research on bacteria, parasites, and other microorganisms. They are playing an important role in protecting public health.

OPHTHALMOLOGY

It deals with the study of the eye. Veterinary ophthalmologists treat eye diseases. They conduct a complete examination of the eye, perform surgeries, and consult with other vets to help prevent issues before they begin.

POULTRY VETERINARY MEDICINE

Poultry veterinarians work with domestic birds like chickens, turkeys, ostrichs, and ducks. These veterinarians work in food production, ensuring meat and eggs are safe for consumption. They can also choose to work with just one species of poultry (chickens, turkeys, quails, ostrich, and ducks). Some veterinarian works on the control sheds of broiler and layer.

PREVENTIVE MEDICINE

Prevention is the greatest health strategy for human beings. It makes perfect sense that it is very effective for animals. Preventive medicine veterinarians work for both animals and humans to detect and control diseases. This is a naturally collaborative area of study that lends itself to employment regulatory medicine, epidemiology, and public health.

RADIOLOGY

Imaging that was once specific to humans is now widely available for animals, but not every veterinarian is fully versed in the appropriate technology. The veterinarian knows well about the procedure of X-rays and ultrasound.

THERIOGENOLOGY

Theriogenology is the study of the reproductive tract of an animal. Theriogenologist responsible for breeding, performing everything from routine pregnancy checks to corrective surgical procedures. Because of their extensive training in animal reproduction, they are particularly important for managing agriculture and protected species populations.

Employment Sector/Industry for Veterinary Doctor/ Veterinarian

Job opportunities for veterinarians are available in both government and private sectors. A vet doctor can also start his clinics/hospitals by providing medical treatment for animals. Veterinary doctors can be employed with:

Private clinics

Hospitals

Laboratories

Slaughterhouses

Shelter houses

Farms and ranches

Social advocacy organizations

Pharmaceutical industry

University lecturer

Animal Nutritional Center as a nutritionist

Food supplement industries

Responsibilities of a Veterinarian

- They are responsible for performing surgery on large and small animals
- Examining animals to diagnose health problems in labs
- Treating and dressing wounds
- Operating medical equipment like computerized tomography (CT) scans, X-ray machines on animals
- Testing for vaccines against diseases
- Vaccinating animals
- Prescribing medication
- Advising animal owners about their pets, treatments, and general care
- Euthanizing animals
- Skills Required

- Clinical skills
- A solid grounding in Medical Science
- Diagnostic skills (with no verbal interaction)
- Lab research skills
- It is the responsibility to create soft skills to deal with upset pet owners
- Understanding of the scientific literature
- They work as a team player (Vet Surgeons work with support staff)
- They should have a full interest in learning modern practices and advanced research and technology facilities

Chapter 4

A Veterinary Medicine Career - Is That Right for You?

If you love animals and science, then you may want to get a veterinarian.

Who are veterinarians and what do they have to do with animals?

Veterinarians are primarily animal doctors who diagnose and prescribe treatment for animals.

Physicians who treat people when they are sick are called doctors and those who treat animals when they are sick or injured are called veterinarians.

What should I study at high school if I want to study to be a vet?

A degree in veterinary science is a very popular and competitive choice, and special skills are required to study it at university. With such stiff competition, good grades, as well as an impressive personal statement and previous work experience, are essential.

You will need to study chemistry and biology first and if some aspirants also study weight physics and mathematics then some universities prefer it. Modules, just like when you get a degree in medicine, are scientific and students must have a strong scientific background to facilitate further study.

There is a good chance that you will have to go through a very competitive interview process. This is more common than ever because your future lecturers will want to know more about what you have done in the past, as well as your passion and commitment to veterinary science.

Veterinary from the USA

Veterinarians are in high demand in Canada, the United States, and many other countries. The scope of careers in veterinary science is huge and is growing rapidly in this age of the modern world. The following are the careers listed below to enhance the career of veterinarians.

Complete undergraduate degree in biological or physical sciences. The undergraduate degree focuses on chemistry, biology, zoology, physiology, microbiology, and anatomy.

Get a Doctor of Veterinary Medicine (DVM) degree from a veterinary school approved by the American Veterinary Medical Association (AVMA). To become a veterinarian, you must have a degree in veterinary science, which includes 4 years of study in veterinary school.

Admission Process

Not all veterinary colleges require a bachelor's degree for admission. Some of these require undergraduate credit hours and pre-veterinary courses in organic chemistry, zoology, biology, and physics.

Entrance examinations in veterinary schools are also offered based on satisfactory scores ie Graduate Record Examination (GRE), Medical Common Admission Test (MCAT), or Veterinary College Admission Test (VCAT).

Famous people who studied veterinary science

Many famous names were first trained as veterinary surgeons before changing career paths. A very famous personality William Hall Macy Jr. - an American actor, screenwriter, teacher, and director in theater, film, and television also liked animals. He studied veterinary medicine at Bethany College in West Virginia. Besides, Olympic Boslia Estrad Radjanovich studied veterinary science at Wahroonga and the University of Sydney.

The Top 10 Reasons to Become a Veterinarian

Do you have a "A" type personality? Are you flexible enough to accept change? Do you have excellent communication skills? Do you have an innate curiosity for learning and veterinary medicine? Do you have a deep love and compassion for all kinds of animals? Do you have an interest in learning sciences? Do you mind getting dirty?

1. Helping Animals

The biggest benefit of a career in veterinary medicine, as a veterinary pathologist, is the opportunity to promote the health and well-being of your patients. You also have the potential to alleviate the suffering of animals that have suffered traumatic injuries or chronic illnesses. Even routine periods and nutritional surgery help animals in your community by reducing overpopulation.

2. Interesting Work

No two days are the same for a veterinarian. You will use a variety of diagnostic tools to examine different types of animals, look at different types of injuries and conditions, and determine the best course of action. You never know what will happen to the clinic on any day.

3. Excellent Salary

Veterinary medicine is one of the animal careers that can offer a high paid salary, although you have to take into account all the educational costs of getting this DVM degree.

4. Community Interaction

Vets meet many members of the community to look after their animals for strength and emergency. They also have the opportunity to educate and advise owners on many important health issues, such as spay/neutering programs and proper nutrition for their animals.

5. Problem-Solving

It takes some detective work to investigate every case, and one of the key virtues of a veterinarian is that he enjoys the challenge. Animals cannot clearly explain what is bothering them, so you have to find out based on physical examination, lab tests, and owner's comments.

6. Professional Independence

Once you start working for an established clinic, you have the option to start your practice, even a mobile practice, which greatly reduces start-up costs. If you are looking to expand the established clinic or if you are considering retiring from other animals, you can become a partner in an established clinic. Most animals have some flexibility in their schedules, especially when they become more stable.

7. Lifetime Learning

Veterinarians never stop learning new things. Education for Pharmaceutical Practice Education to renew your license requires ongoing education hours, and most animals want to learn new techniques and innovations even when there is no official need.

The industry is constantly evolving, and it's important to keep up to date so that you can provide the best possible care for your clients. Vets can obtain board certification in several areas requiring additional training and experience in specialized areas.

8. Career Options

You can use your veterinary background to change multiple roles with other organizations, such as veterinary pharmaceutical sales companies, feed companies, wildlife agencies, laboratories, educational institutions, or the military. Corporate weights, in particular, earn top dollars and operate during normal business hours. You don't have to limit yourself to traditional private practice by seeing patients every day.

9. Professional Community

Veterinarians have the opportunity to lead a team of animal lovers, including veterinary technicians, kennel attendants, and office staff. It makes a difference when all the employees in an office enjoy what they do for a living, and, in the process, people are committed to helping animals.

10. Animal Dream Job

Animal medicine is by far the most popular dream job for animal lovers, and many children begin to express their interest in this career path at a very young age. If you have the drive, the degree, and the desire to work with animals, veterinary medicine may be the best job for you.

Chapter 5
A Typical Day in the Life of a Veterinarian

A veterinarian has a challenging and rewarding career. It can be ideal for someone who enjoys critical thinking, is not afraid of hard work, and loves animals! Learn what to look for and tactics to help ease the way.

I get it a lot It seems like every time I meet a new group of people, I hear it from at least one of them. But I don't mind because,

1) I've always wanted to be a veterinarian,

2) It is a great job, and

3) I think it's great to be a veterinarian.

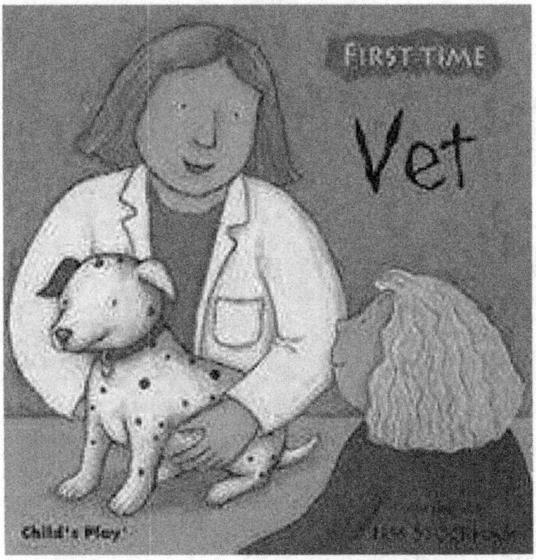

The Day Begins

Every animal in the hospital, whether coming for surgery or if it was not recovering from the night before, has undergone a physical examination so that the doctor can plan treatment and note any findings. Physical examination includes taking a date from the owner, petting the pet, listening to the heart and lungs, and feeling the sensation of something unusual in the body, such as a mass or lump.

Animals undergoing surgery on this day usually enter early in the morning. Once admitted, blood samples are made to the pet for blood work before surgery. Blood work provides the doctor with information about how the body works internally, information that is not possible with just a physical examination. After the vet has examined the lab work, the pet can be prepared for surgery.

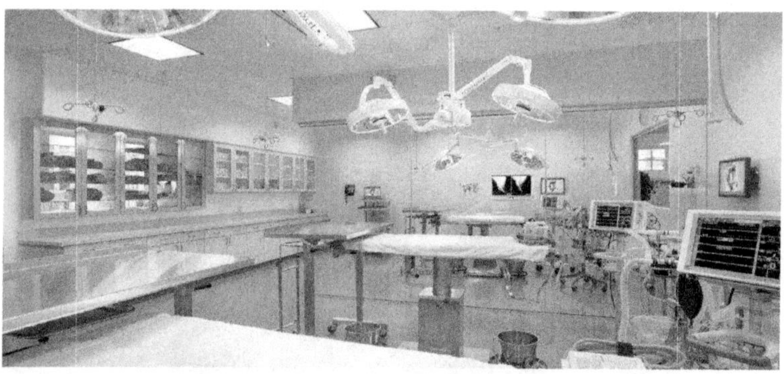

In the morning, the surgical procedure allows the patient to recover throughout the day so that plenty of staff can monitor the progress. After-hours appointments include visits to new dogs or kittens, vaccinations, sick visits where pets are not recovering, and everything in between! An essential and difficult appointment that all veterinarians see to help pets move from euthanasia. These appointments are also scheduled during the day, but can also be made in an emergency.

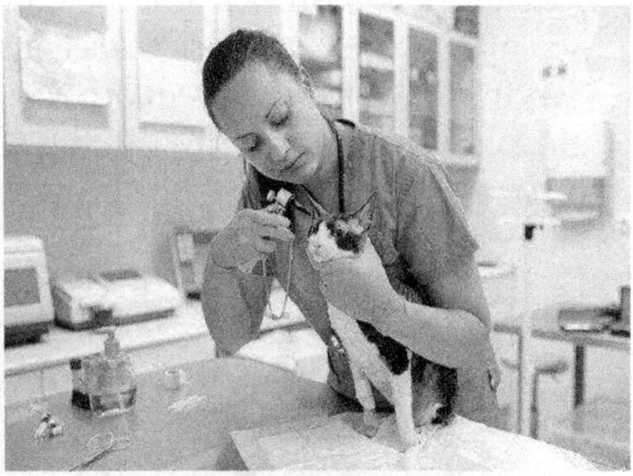

Lunchtime

Most clinics pause appointments at lunchtime, not only for nourishment but also for catch-up play. Employees at the bustling clinic use phone calls this time around to check on animals that have been hospitalized and are recovering from anesthesia and hope to have lunch sometime. Emergencies can pass through the door at any time of the day and require immediate attention. As a result, all veterinary team members should practice good time management. If there are several veterinarians in an office, the office is open at lunchtime, and each doctor will take a break from his or her surprise.

Afternoon

Surgery in the upper part of the afternoon is usually spent on seeing more appointments and dismissals of patients.

If pets are seen during the visit and they are very sick or irritable, the doctor will recommend that the owner be taken to an emergency hospital, where a veterinary team is available around the clock to monitor and arrange treatment. Sick pets that are shown during appointments usually have lab work and X-rays in the hospital to find out why the "pet" is sick because of them. Although veterinary technicians and nurses run the lab or take X-rays, the doctor has still looked at other appointments. When the results of these tests come back, a big part of the veterinarian's job is to explain the results to the pet owner and plan the treatment. Talking to pet owners about pet diseases is a big part of a veterinarian's day.

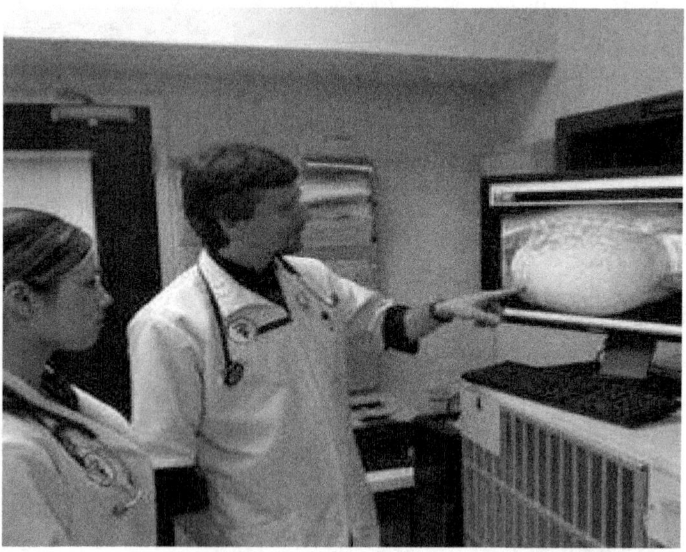

Afternoon breaks are usually available to return phone calls, allow prescriptions, and finalize medical notes before the end of the day.

Duties of Veterinarians

Veterinarians typically do the following:

- Examine animals to diagnose their health problems
- Treat and dress wounds
- Perform surgery on animals
- Test for and vaccinate against diseases
- Operate medical equipment, such as x-ray machines
- Advise animal owners about general care, medical conditions, and treatments
- Prescribe medication
- Euthanize animals

Chapter 6

Pros and Cons of Becoming a Vet

If you are a caring person who loves animals, a career as a doctor may just be the job for you.

However, while there is no denying that a lot of animal status can be achieved if you are seriously considering a career in the veterinary industry, it is important to consider all professionals.

Opportunity to work with your four-legged friends, help them recover when they are sick, vaccinate against diseases, and teach pet owners how the best care to be taken for their fur sounds as if there is no great work. But, like any character, there are ups and downs. It takes years of training to become a vet. Once in the role, you are expected to work long hours. Yes, the pay can be quite decent but let's not forget the emotional roller coaster dealing with sick and injured animals.

So, if you are looking to pursue your career as a vet, read on to discover some key pros and cons.

A career as a vet: PROS

You'll have a job that you love.

Becoming a veterinarian means you will be surrounded by different animals. Maybe one day you'll be working with small, sharp-edged dogs. The next day you will be treating big cows or horses. You will face a lot of challenges, but all of them can be worth it because you are following your passion and working in a job that suits your values and interests.

You'll have the chance to help animals

Becoming a veterinarian gives you the skills and knowledge you need to treat and rehabilitate dogs, cats, and other animals. This is a very rewarding part of the job: helping a creature who came to your clinic in a bad condition and using their abilities to improve their health and well-being.

Rewarding

Becoming a vet can be a wonderful experience. Diagnosing, treating, and helping our dear friend feel better can be both satisfying and rewarding. As a vet, you can educate pet owners and human caregivers about the precautions they can take to promote maximum animal health.

High demand

Australia and the US have one of the highest rates of pet ownership in the world. More than 62% of households have pets in Australia. As a result, there should be a lot of demand for vets. Indeed, news reports in the last year have referred to the limited number of vets and the high number of roles available.

Versatile

A career as a doctor involves more than just treating sick and injured animals. The role is focused on education and customer service, as well as personal and business development.

If you run your veterinary practice, you will need to hire and manage staff services and help with training and professional development.

Good salary

Being a vet isn't a badly paid job for all incoming students in this field. The average salary for a veterinarian is $101404 per year in the United States.

Working with animals

Of course, if you love animals, the best part of working as an animal is probably spending the day with animals.

A career as a vet: CONS

Lengthy training

To become a veterinarian, you need proper training. This is usually a veterinary science degree, which takes five years of full-time study.

You'll struggle for work-life balance

More likely than not, you can still find yourself working long hours and meeting on call even after your workday is over. This is especially true if you live in a small town that does not have many animal experts. As a result, you may find it difficult to balance your work and family life, and you may experience permanent fatigue and loss of work.

Demanding work

Being a vet requires physical and mental help. You are likely to work long hours, especially if you are on the call. You may even need to work on the weekends and most jobs require you to stand, lift, and bend on your own feet.

There's also the risk of personal injury. Animals that are sick, injured, or distressed can be bitten. Indeed, a study into the prevalence of injuries sustained by Australian veterinarians revealed that of 2800 veterinarians, over half (51%) reported a significant work-related injury during their career. Dog and cat bites, as well as musculoskeletal injuries, were common.

Dealing with sickness

Although living with animals every day seems like a great career, many of the animals you encounter are very sick. Treating injured animals can be extremely emotional and stressful. Besides, it can cause blood, mucus, infections, and unpleasant odors to deal with. Being a vet is not a charming job!

Euthanasia

There is no denying the emotional toll of euthanasia on vets. The grief of pet owners can have a significant and devastating effect on the stress and anxiety associated with euthanasing and dealing with animals regularly.

Anyone wanting a career as a vet must recognize the potential impact of euthanasia know the warning signs to look out for and be aware of helpful ways in which to deal with the emotional side of performing euthanasia.

Compassion fatigue

Due to the emotional state of the heart and the regular trauma, he can be emotionally damaged. Although not unique to vets, empathy fatigue is common in people who work in veterinary practice. Being aware of the condition, the symptoms, and the risk factors is an important part of being a vet.

You'll struggle for work-life balance

More likely than not, you can still find yourself working long hours and meeting on call even after your workday is over. This is especially true if you live in a small town that does not have many animal experts. As a result, you may find it difficult to balance your work and family life, and you may experience permanent fatigue and loss of work.

Chapter 7

How to Become a Veterinary Assistant

Do you have what it takes?

Veterinary assistants take care of animals under the supervision of a veterinary doctor or veterinary technician. They are responsible for feeding, bathing, and exercising the animals and they stop them during examinations and treatment.

Veterinary assistants, sometimes perform lab work, such as drawing blood and collecting urine samples. In 2016, about 83,800 animal assistants worked in the United States, and about 85% of them worked for veterinary services.

The biggest challenge for veterinary assistant students is to understand the need for superior customer service skills as well as animal handling skills.

Veterinary assistants play a major role in helping veterinarians perform surgery and other procedures. They prepare equipment and transfer surgical instruments and equipment to veterinarians during surgery and stop or restrain the animal during testing and other procedures.

Veterinary assistants must demonstrate emotional strength, resilience, and maturity in dealing with abused animals or those who cannot return to a decent standard of living. The skills of great people are also important, as animal helpers are often the first point of contact for distressed animal owners.

A veterinary assistant also knows about medicine a little bit. In the absence of a vet doctor, an assistant can check the patient and do all the tests that he studied in his education career. He also helps the vet in restraining large animals such as horses and cattle. An assistant can also work in the field to earn. It is a good job for all the kids who are interested in animal sciences.

Veterinary Assistant Duties & Responsibilities

- Veterinary assistants perform all aspects of daily pet care and in the absence of a vet doctor, they also handle the clinic.
- Feed animals and monitor whether they're eating.
- Bathing pets when necessary.
- Exercise the animals.
- Assist veterinarians and vet technicians with lab work.
- Clean, sterilize, and maintain kennels, operating rooms, examining rooms, cages, and surgical equipment.
- Comfort and restrain pets during examinations and care.
- Provide first aid to pets in an emergency, stabilizing them until a doctor can take over.
- Administer medications to pets.
- Perform some clerical duties.

Veterinary hospitals and clinics employ mostly veterinary assistants, but some work in colleges, universities, and research programs.

Veterinary Assistant Salary

Those vet assistants who work at colleges and professional schools are the most highly paid.

Median Annual Salary: $27,540 ($13.24/hour)

Top 10% Annual Salary: More than $38,890 ($18.70/hour)

Bottom 10% Annual Salary: Less than $19,950 ($9.59/hour)

Education, Training & Certification

This profession does not require higher education for a job, but you will need a lot of training to handle all types of cases at the clinic. In veterinary sciences, you will have to practice a lot to become a good assistant.

Education: You will need a high school or equivalent diploma for the job, as opposed to a veterinary technician who must complete a two-year post-secondary program in veterinary technology.

Training: Most employers provide on-the-job job training, but some will only employ people with professional experience working with animals.

Veterinary Assistant Skills & Competencies

The following soft skills - Personal traits with which you were either born or gained through life experiences are the key to your success in this field.

- A good veterinary assistant has strong listening skills that are necessary to understand and follow veterinarians' and veterinary technicians' instructions.
- The ability to see changes in animals' conditions will permit you to take appropriate action.
- Veterinary assistants need a strong desire to help others during the service.
- This skill will allow you to decide what your options are when making decisions or solving problems, evaluate them, and then make a choice with a very promising outcome.
- You just have to be more discriminating with the help you render toward other people.

Job Outlook

The Bureau of Labor Statistics predicts that employment will grow above average for all occupations between 2016 and 2026, about 19%. BLS expects to increase consumer spending on pets and their care.

Work Environment

Whether you work in the veterinary office, at school, or in research, you will spend most of your time in kennels, exterior walls, labs, and operating rooms. Some of your patients may be angry or frightened. You may be at risk for bites or itching, although wearing protective clothing and apparel can help prevent it.

Work can sometimes be sad and unpleasant. You have to help the veterinarians when you please the animals dispose of the remains and comfort the grieving owners. Some of your patients may be abusive or very ill.

Work Schedule

This job lends itself to part-time. About 40% of veterinary assistants worked less than 40 hours a week in 2016. Some may need to work on weekends, holidays, and nights, however, to take care of pets who cannot go to their families' homes while recovering.

How long does it take to become a veterinarian assistant?

Associate-level programs typically take two years or less to complete, while bachelor's degrees take four years. The Veterinary Assistant Certificate program can usually be completed in a year or less.

Is being a vet assistant hard?

Jobs sometimes require stress and physical demands. Animals get sick at all times of the day and night and need care, so experienced assistants often work on holidays, nights, and weekends. Assistants sometimes have to move large animals and treat them.

How much does veterinary assistant school cost?

Program length: self-speed; Students can complete the program in 6 or 12 months (depending on the program) from the time of enrollment. Tuition costs: ‹ 2,080$ - 2,390$ (tuition fees may change at any time).

Can you be a vet assistant without a degree?

There is no formal educational requirement to become a veterinary assistant, although in most cases people will earn a high school diploma.

Chapter 8

How Kids Can Help Animals!

What do you want to be in the future when you grow up? Your answer perhaps changes every day. Or maybe someone wants something special for you and you're already moving towards it. Whatever your wishes may be, achieving those goals does not have to start quickly. So every week, we'll be highlighting a specific career, which includes everything in each type of class that you should take step by step on the doorstep. We hope this encourages you to think about your plans so that one day you can go to the job of your dreams.

How Kids Can Help Animals!

What's The Big Deal?

Some animals are the most populous in the world, such as cats and dogs. Wherever you live, you may find a lost dog or cat roaming the streets. You may be worried that they may be hit by a car. Fortunately, at least some of these animals have homes.

But no one owns wild animals. His house is outside in the forest. They depend on nature for food and shelter. But even that is not always safe for them!

Some of these wild animals are endangered or extinct. One of the endangered species is a species that is so small that it is in danger of extinction. Once a species is endangered, it can take many years to bring it back to normal. If not, it may disappear. Extinction occurs when a species dies forever, that is, there is no one left on Earth.

While some of this happens naturally, much of it is now due to humans! All over the world, our pollution, hunting, and deforestation threaten homes and food sources for wildlife.

This is a huge problem! We need to be aware of the issues created for animals and us, especially how you can help!

Did You Know?

- There are more than 3,000 endangered species in the world.
- Currently, 99% of the endangered species are endangered by human activities.
- By 2025, 20 of all animal species could be gone forever.
- By 2050, 30 to 50 of all species may be extinct.
- There are more than 100,000 species of plants and animals in the freshwater ecosystem. They are one of the most endangered habitats in the world!
- The World Wildlife Organization protects wildlife such as pandas, whales, rhinos, polar bears, and large cats.
- Due to the abuse of cats and dogs, about 2.7 million animals fall asleep every year.

What Can You Do?

Although there are many difficulties, there are many other ways you can help! Even if you don't live close to the animals yourself! Here are some ways in which you can improve your animal life:

Do something small:

Tell your friends! Share why you decided to help animals and encourage them to do so.

Keep up-to-date on all the news about animals who need your help!

Take a stand against animal testing and only buy products that are free from cruelty.

Visit a national wildlife refuge, park, or other open space. Protected lands provide habitat for many climatic life, birds, fish, and plants. Volunteer at your local nature center.

Do something big

Volunteer at your local animal shelter! Whether you walk dogs, clean cups of water, or hang signs, they have a job for you. You can make a big difference in the lives of stray dogs, cats, and other animals!

Many organizations and zoos have volunteer programs. You can help clean up the beaches or save the wildlife.

You and your classmates can adopt an animal from a wildlife conservation organization. You can help protect them by embracing a wild animal like a bison, or by donating them to a prairie, like a wild place.

Write to your politicians to speak out against poaching, which is the illegal hunting of wild animals. (You can write a letter to the Secretary of State for the American Wildlife Conservation Society)

Get Inspired!

Remember you are not alone! Kids all over the world like you are making a difference and you can too! You should study more which will help you make a better tomorrow.

Chapter 9

College of Veterinary Medicine - DVM Degree

Essential skills and abilities

The Doctor of Veterinary Medicine degree indicates that the holder is ready to enter the practice of veterinary medicine with or without postgraduate study. All veterinary students must have extensive scientific knowledge and technical expertise so that they can work independently in a wide range of clinical, research, and other fields.

Candidates for the DVM degree must demonstrate the necessary skills and abilities to meet the overall curriculum and course-specific requirements. Besides, students should be able to work safely and efficiently in multiple environments such as classrooms, laboratories, examinations, large and small animal clinics, and a variety of animal environments. The discovery of chemicals (such as drugs, antibiotics,

anesthetics, and tissue fixatives) and pathogens is inevitable during veterinary school and beyond.

Veterinarians operate under a code of ethics and professional conduct that forms a social contract between the profession and society. This degree is awarded only when the student has a satisfactory mastery of the necessary scientific and medical knowledge as well as technical skills, while professional skills, attitudes, and behaviors are also obtained from any professional specialist degree. Throughout the curriculum, students should demonstrate a high level of compassion for all animals and people, have excellent mutual and communication skills, high moral and ethical standards, and an incentive to serve, and be expected of them. They come from all ethnic, social, cultural, and religious backgrounds.

Essential Requirements

The following information will acquaint applicants and students with expectations, abilities, and attitudes to meet curriculum and career needs. It does not matter if an individual student intends to pursue only a narrow portion of clinical medicine practice or pursue a non-clinical career, the requirement that all veterinary students receive the required curriculum through faculty and qualify.

College of Veterinary Medicine has a moral responsibility to protect patients and clients with whom students and veterinarians interact and interrelate. The safety and well-being of the patient and the client are essential factors in establishing, promoting, and strengthening the physical, cognitive, and emotional abilities of the candidates for graduation. Candidates for a DVM degree should be able to incorporate various tactile, visual, and auditory stimuli from their environment and then process this information based on their knowledge and experience and finally give appropriate answers that include both verbal communication and numerous bodily functions. Candidates for the DVM degree must demonstrate skills and abilities in five areas:

- Observation
- Communication
- Motor
- intellectual (conceptual, integration, and quantitative)
- behavioral and social

Observation

The candidate should be able to observe and review required demonstrations and experiments, including anatomical denial, microscopic analysis, animal/patient demonstrations, and limited to radiographic and other graphic and diagnostic images. The candidate must be able to take a close look at a patient's distance and evaluate the results. She / He must understand and interpret the symptoms of fear, aggression, and other potentially dangerous behaviors caused by different types of animals. Observation requires the active use of vision, hearing, and somatosensory in often complex situations in the veterinary healthcare environment.

Communication

The candidate must be able to convey information, build relationships, provide explanations, and describe changes in behavior, activity, and currency. Communication includes not only speech, but also the interpretation of unconventional gestures, and reading and writing in English. The candidate should be able to communicate effectively, efficiently, and on time with all members of the healthcare team.

Motor Function

A candidate must have sufficient motor skills to use scientific and diagnostic instruments, to carry out animal restraint, and to perform essential diagnostic procedures, including palpation, and other components of a physical exam on live animals, to perform surgical procedures.

A candidate should be able to perform motor movements so that it is reasonably necessary to provide general care, surgery, and emergency treatment to patients of all species. Besides, the candidate should be able to avoid physically dangerous contact with animal patients. Such functions require coordination between both overall and fine muscle movements, balance, and active use of the senses of vision, vision, and hearing.

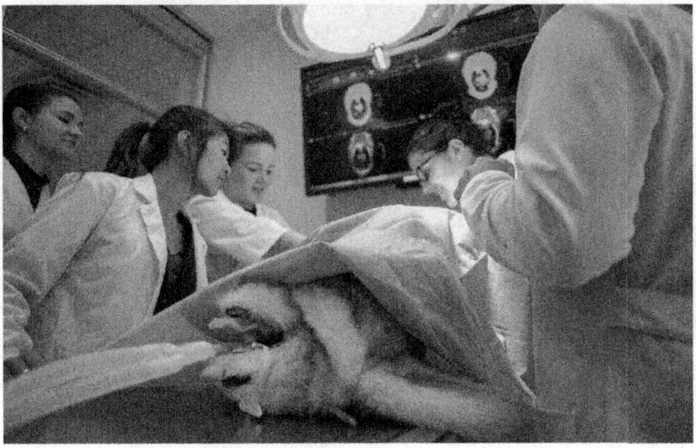

Intellectual (Conceptual, Integrative, and Quantitative)

Problem-solving, an important veterinary skill, requires that the candidate be able to efficiently and accurately obtain, retrieve, analyze, integrate, and synthesize information from a variety of sources. Besides, the candidate must have the ability to accurately measure and calculate, understand triangular relationships, and understand the local relationships of the structure.

Candidates should be able to formulate and evaluate assumptions that enable them to diagnose and treat patients effectively and timely in a variety of medical conditions. In many cases, these decisions and appropriate diagnostic and treatment measures are time-sensitive. Therefore, candidates must demonstrate skills, knowledge, and abilities to handle multiple situations simultaneously.

Behavioral and Social Attributes

A candidate must use his / her intellectual abilities to the fullest, use good judgment, quickly complete those responsible for diagnosing and caring for patients, and interact with his or her companions, peers, staff, colleagues, and clients must be able to build effective relationships.

She/ he should be able to work effectively as a member of the healthcare team and be able to bear the taxing workload physically and emotionally, effectively under stress, to work, and to show flexibility and functionality in the face of internal uncertainty.

Candidates need to be able to communicate clearly and informally to clients and staff in a timely and effective manner, using both oral and written forms. She/ he should understand the legal and ethical aspects of the practice of veterinary medicine, and work within both the law and ethical standards of the veterinary profession.

The candidate is expected to demonstrate a high commitment to professional conduct which includes competence, empathy, integrity, lifelong learning, concern for others, mutual abilities, collective, interest, and promotion of public interest. But not limited to them.

Chapter 10

Some Important Terminologies, Helpful in Veterinary Sciences

Bull	mature male cattle
Steer	castrated male cattle
Heifer	female cattle that have not calved
Cow	mature female cattle
Calf	young cattle
9 months	the gestation period of cattle
Boar	mature male swine
Barrow	castrated male swine
Gilt	female swine that has not farrowed
Sow	mature female swine
Piglet	newborn swine
3 months	gestation of swine
Ram	mature male sheep
Wether	castrated male sheep/goat
Ewe	female sheep
Lamb	young sheep
5 months	the gestation of sheep/goats
Billy	mature male goat
Doe	mature female goat/rabbit
Kidding	giving birth-goats
Calving	giving birth-cattle
Farrowing	giving birth-swine
Lambing	giving birth-sheep
Foaling	giving birth-horses
Hatching	giving birth-poultry
Kindling	giving birth-rabbits

Foal	newborn horse
Colt	immature male horse
Stallion	mature male horse
Gelding	castrated male horse
Filly	immature female horse
Mare	mature female horse

Gene

DNA, which is located on a chromosome, which offspring will inherit.

Breed

An animal that has been selected for certain characteristics and that is produced with the characteristics.

A.I. (Artificial Insemination)

The procedure for placing semen in the reproductive tract of a female animal through means other than the natural mating act in the hopes of causing a pregnancy.

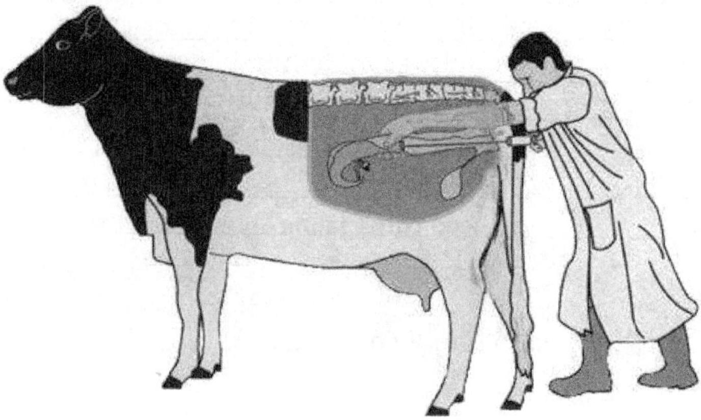

BST (Bovine Somatotropin)

Growth hormone in cattle. Produced and secreted by the anterior pituitary gland, acts on various target tissues throughout the body. Primarily, works through the second growth hormone. Increases milk production dramatically, presumably by increasing nutrient availability to the secretory cells, or by increasing the production of milk components directly.

Colostrum

Specialized milk is produced in the early days following parturition to provide extra nutrients and immune function to the young. It is higher in vitamins, minerals, and protein compared with normal milk and generally carries antibodies to aid the young in developing an immune response against potential antigens.

Lactation The process of producing milk.

Conception When the sperm fertilizes the ovum.

Estrous Cycle Time from one estrus to the next.

Estrus Period of sexual receptivity in the female.

Seasonal Polyestrous; An animal, that has extraneous cycles according to season.

The anestrous period is when a female does not have estrous cycles.

Forage Fiber containing feeds like grass or hay; can be grazed or harvested for feeding; it contains at least 18% fiber and has high digestible energy > 70%.

Heritability What the offspring inherit from their parents. (A measure of the proportion of phenotypic variation that is caused by additive gene effects. The proportion of differences between individuals that is genetic.)

Spontaneous Mutation Chemical change in a gene, which occurs spontaneously.

Ad libidum Having feed available at all times.

Omnivores are Animals that eat both plant and animal-based foods.

Withdrawal Times

The period after a drug is administered to an animal that the milk or meat from that animal must not be used for human food.

Cross-fostering Moving young from their dam (mother) and placing them with another female for rearing (raising and feeding).

Colic A digestive disturbance involving severe contractions, twisting, or obstructions in the digestive tract.

Monogastric Having only one stomach. A term used to differentiate between animals that have a rumen and those that don't.

Ruminant One stomach with four compartments: rumen, reticulum, omasum, and abomasum.

Palatability Acceptability of a feed or ration to livestock. Influenced by taste, texture, form of feed, dustiness, and several other factors.

Wean Remove offspring from the dam (mother) and prevent them from nursing.

Avian About poultry and/or fowl.

Brooder A device with controlled heat and light used to warm chicks from the day of hatch to approximately 5 weeks of age. The heat is usually contained in a large reflector or hover under which the birds congregate.

Candling Inspection of the inside of an intact egg with light to detect defects. Incubating eggs can also be tested for dead germs and infertile eggs.

Game Birds

Fowl for which there is an established hunting season. Also, refers to fighting chickens.

Incubator

A machine that provides the environmental conditions that encourage embryonic development.

Molting

The shedding of feathers by chickens. Usually, egg-laying is reduced or stopped at molting.

Plumage The total body feathering of poultry.

Shelf-life The period of freshness and wholesomeness of food items. In poultry, the length of time fresh-dressed, iced, packed poultry can be held without freezing.

AAFCO (Association of American Feed Control Officials)

The basic function of AAFCO is to provide a mechanism for developing and implementing uniform and equitable laws, regulations, standards, and enforcement policies for regulating the manufacture, distribution, and sale of animal feeds; resulting in safe, effective, and useful feeds.

Cattle genus and species? **Bos Taurus/Bos indicus**

Swine genus and species? **Sus scrofa**

Sheep genus and species? **Ovies aries**

Horse genus and species? **Equus caballus**

Poultry genus and species? **Gallus Domestica**

Dog genus and species? **Canis lupus**

Cat genus and species? **Felis catus**

Some subjects you will be taught in DVM

Anatomy

Anatomy is the branch of biology concerned with the study of the structure of organisms and their parts. Anatomy is a branch of natural science that deals with the structural organization of living things.

Physiology

is the scientific study of functions and mechanisms in a living system. As a sub-discipline of biology, physiology focuses on how organisms, organ systems, individual organs, cells, and biomolecules carry out the chemical and physical functions in a living system.

Pathology

Pathology is the study of the causes and effects of disease or injury. The word pathology also refers to the study of disease in general, incorporating a wide range of biology research fields, and medical and veterinary practices.

Histology

It also known as microscopic anatomy or microanatomy, is the branch of biology that studies the microscopic anatomy of biological tissues.

Parasitology

Parasitology is the study of parasites, their hosts, and the relationship between them.

Microbiology

Microbiology is the study of microorganisms, those being unicellular, multicellular, or acellular.

Biochemistry

Biochemistry or biological chemistry is the study of chemical processes within and relating to living organisms. A sub-discipline of both chemistry and biology, biochemistry may be divided into three fields: structural biology, enzymology, and metabolism.

Statistics

Statistics is the discipline that concerns the collection, organization, analysis, interpretation, and presentation of data.

Printed in Dunstable, United Kingdom

74677824R00047